CCSS Genre Realistic Fiction

Essential Question
How can we take responsibility?

The Hardest Lesson

by Jesse Anna Bornemann
illustrated by Carl Pearce

Chapter 1
The Geography Bee. 2

Chapter 2
The Lie 8

Chapter 3
A Difficult Confession 12

Respond to Reading. 16

PAIRED READ Training Wheels 17

Focus on Literary Elements 20

 # The Geography Bee

"Please, Mom, just one more time?" Timothy pleaded, pushing a thick stack of index cards across the kitchen table toward his mother.

"Honey, if you stay up much later, you'll fall asleep on the stage tomorrow," said Mom, looking concerned.

Timothy shook his head. If there was one thing he knew for sure, it was that he'd be wide awake for the Geography Bee. He had been anticipating it for months, practically since the first day of sixth grade. Well, maybe not that long, but at least since he'd aced the qualifying test and advanced to the final school-wide round. Only one other kid in his class, Marcus Braylock, had scored a perfect 100% on the test. Now, Timothy and Marcus would represent Mr. Maxwell's class against the other three sixth-grade classes.

"The capital of Poland is Warsaw, and the capital of Portugal is Lisbon," Timothy said, inching the cards closer to his mother.

"Come on, just imagine how great two trophies will look above the fireplace!" Timothy continued hopefully.

Timothy's sister, Deanna, had won the title of Bee champion four years ago, and even though Timothy had only been in second grade at the time, he vividly remembered how proud his parents had been. Every time he went into the living room to watch television or read a book, Deanna's gold statue stared down at him from the mantel.

"And now it's my turn," Timothy thought.

"A couple more, then bedtime," Mom said firmly, taking two cards from the top of the pile. "The capital of Austria is …?" she read aloud.

Timothy thought for a moment. Then it came to him. "Vienna!"

"And Ireland?" Mom continued.

Timothy grinned. "Easy … Dublin!"

The next morning Timothy woke to a delicious smell filling the apartment, and the scent drew him out of bed. Dad had made Belgian waffles in honor of European geography.

"Eat quickly, though, or you'll miss the bus," Mom said. "Deanna already left for school, but she said to break a leg."

Wishing he had set his alarm for slightly earlier, Timothy inhaled the waffles and then sprinted for the shower.

"And what is the capital of Belgium?" Mom quizzed when Timothy was showered and dressed.

"Brussels!" Timothy replied. He grabbed his backpack and dashed for the door.

That morning the traffic was crawling, the vehicles inching their way forward bumper to bumper. When the bus finally pulled up to the school, Timothy climbed out and rushed to the gymnasium, which was decorated wall-to-wall with the colorful flags of each European country. From his chair on the stage, Timothy gazed at each bright rectangle, trying to distract himself from the crowd seated below.

For the first round of the Bee, he would take turns with his seven competitors labeling countries on a large blank map of Europe. Each correctly labeled country would earn a point. In the second round, Principal Harris would name a European country, and the first student to buzz in with the capital city would gain a point. The class with the highest point total was to receive a pizza party. As much as Timothy liked pizza, he really wanted the individual grand prize—the trophy.

Principal Harris stepped up to the podium. "Lydia, please label Italy," she instructed. Most of the kids groaned; even a first grader would know Italy from its boot shape.

However, by the end of the first round, Timothy and Lydia were tied for the lead, with Marcus in second place.

"Well, it's anybody's game after round one," Principal Harris said, smiling. "And now, here is the first question in round two. Can anyone tell me the capital city of Portugal?"

Hardly pausing to blink or breathe, Timothy pressed his buzzer and blurted out Lisbon as the answer.

When Principal Harris confirmed that he was correct, Timothy pumped his fist in silent victory, keeping his arm next to his seat so that no one could see.

Within minutes, Timothy and Lydia were tied again, but then he overtook her on Switzerland. Mr. Maxwell's class cheered, while Lydia's teacher, Mrs. Ellenbaum, attempted to silence the grumbles of displeasure from her students.

"We're coming to the end, folks," Principal Harris said, shooting a disapproving glance at a couple of particularly rowdy boys. "The next country is Sweden."

Before Timothy had time to react, Lydia's buzzer went off. He tried hard to keep the smile off his face when she incorrectly answered Oslo.

"No, I'm sorry, Lydia, that is not correct," Principal Harris said. "Would someone else like to try?"

Timothy shut his eyes and visualized his flashcards, but before he could remember the answer, another buzzer rang.

"Stockholm," Marcus said triumphantly.

Now Marcus and Timothy were tied, and the digital clock on the wall showed that less than a minute remained before the final bell. An expectant hush fell over the gymnasium—the tension was palpable.

"OK, here is the last question," Principal Harris said. "Can any of you tell me what is the capital city of … Belgium?"

In a rush, Timothy pressed his buzzer—but a shrill beep came from several seats down. Timothy couldn't believe it—Marcus must have gotten in less than a second before him. But maybe he'd pick the wrong city?

"Brussels!" exclaimed Marcus confidently.

Timothy's classmates leapt to their feet and applauded, but they weren't clapping for him.

"Mr. Maxwell's class has won the Geography Bee, and the winner of the individual grand prize is Marcus Braylock!" Principal Harris said, leaving the podium to shake Marcus's hand. Mr. Maxwell ducked behind the stage curtain and emerged with the gleaming trophy, which he presented to Marcus. The new champion held the trophy over his head, like a star athlete.

Timothy hunched in his chair, unable to move. His body felt numb, and he was certain he'd never eat waffles again.

Chapter 2 The Lie

The next day at lunchtime, three piping hot pizzas arrived at Mr. Maxwell's classroom door, right on schedule.

"Mmmmm ... victory smells like pizza," Marcus murmured, and everyone laughed—except for Timothy. That morning, he had packed his own lunch of a peanut butter sandwich and some carrot sticks. He'd rather eat mud than celebrate Marcus's win with pizza.

"Are you gonna eat by yourself?" Timothy's friend Josh asked sympathetically when he saw him take out his lunch bag.

Timothy nodded at Josh, then scowled as he watched Marcus lean against a window, surrounded by adoring fans.

"It was a really close contest, and I thought you had it in the bag," Josh said. He bit into a triangle of pizza, and Timothy watched as he twirled a string of cheese around his fingers.

"Hey, man!" Marcus said, looking straight at Timothy—much to Timothy's surprise. Breaking away from his classmates, Marcus strode to Timothy's desk, arm outstretched for a fist bump.

"Congratulations to both of us—none of the other classes stood a chance!"

"Whatever," Timothy muttered, keeping his eyes on his sandwich.

When Mr. Maxwell asked for the class to start finishing off the pizzas, Timothy got up and tossed his mostly uneaten lunch in the trash.

"Please open your science books to page 119," Mr. Maxwell said once the last paper plates and napkins had been thrown out. "If you remember, a few days ago we talked about the three different states of matter: solid, liquid, and gas. All of these states can be represented in the water cycle."

It wasn't hard to see that at least half of the class was still in party mode. A few kids dutifully followed along in their textbooks, but Timothy observed that most were fidgeting in their seats, gazing out the window, or doodling aimlessly. Marcus appeared to be drawing a racing car.

"Who can tell me the stages of the water cycle?" Mr. Maxwell asked.

Timothy raised his hand, but Mr. Maxwell had spied Marcus's artwork and asked Marcus instead.

Marcus dropped his pencil and looked up. With pleasure, Timothy noticed that Marcus's ears were turning a deep red.

"Um ... photosynthesis?" Marcus said in a tiny voice.

The class burst out laughing, and Timothy nearly fell off his chair. Minutes ago, everyone had been ready to crown Marcus king of the sixth grade, but now things were very different.

In giddy delight, Timothy exclaimed, "Not so smart now that the answers aren't written on your hand!" Several kids turned around to stare at him, including Marcus, and Timothy immediately wished he could swallow his words.

"What do you mean by that?" Marcus sputtered.

What *did* he mean, exactly? Timothy looked at Mr. Maxwell, hoping the teacher would somehow help him out, but he was busy silencing other students, who were still hooting and guffawing.

"I just, well ... I saw you write the European capitals on your hand before the Geography Bee," Timothy said.

Marcus gasped and exclaimed, "That's a lie!"

It was a total lie, and Timothy felt ill. Ashamed and miserable, he hid his face behind his science book while Mr. Maxwell quieted the class.

For the rest of the day, Timothy was careful not to look in Marcus's direction. When the final bell rang at last, he shoved his books into his backpack and bolted for the bus.

For most of the weekend, Timothy didn't leave his bedroom. Thinking that he was still glum about the Geography Bee, his family tried to lift his spirits, and on Sunday night his parents ordered Chinese takeout from Timothy's favorite restaurant. Deanna let him have her fortune cookie, but good fortune was the last thing he deserved. He half expected the little slip of paper in the cookie to read: "Honesty is the best policy," or, more straightforwardly, "You will regret your actions."

That night, Timothy slept fitfully. He dreamed that he was playing baseball with Marcus on the field behind the teachers' lounge, and just as Timothy was about to slide into home plate, it started to rain. At first, it was just drizzling, but soon it began to pour. The spheres falling from the sky were all out of proportion with the clouds, though, and with a shudder Timothy realized that the large, green balls weren't rain—they were sprouts. *Brussels* sprouts.

Chapter 3
A Difficult Confession

"Maybe everyone has forgotten what happened on Friday," Timothy thought as he reluctantly boarded the school bus on Monday morning. He knew this was highly unlikely, so in desperation he turned to another idea: maybe Marcus really did cheat during the Geography Bee. After all, how else could he have gotten that final point so quickly? And when had Marcus ever won a contest in class, anyway? What were the odds of Marcus beating some of the smartest kids in the whole sixth grade?

By the time he was walking into Mr. Maxwell's classroom, Timothy had decided that, yes, Marcus must have cheated. Timothy held his head high and forced himself to smile as he strolled casually between the rows and sat down at his desk.

Timothy waited anxiously as the morning dragged by. In math, the lesson was about improper fractions, and one of the problems involved pizza. Out of the corner of his eye, Timothy saw a couple of girls whisper to each other and snicker. Nervously, he waited for someone to crack a joke at Marcus's expense. Marcus must have anticipated the same thing because, as Timothy watched him, he sank lower in his seat.

Josh winked at Timothy, but nothing happened.

The last class before lunch was Language Arts.

"Flip to page 108, and you'll see that each vocabulary word has the prefix *con-*," Mr. Maxwell said.

"*Con-* often means 'together' or 'with,'" Mr. Maxwell explained. "So, for instance, when two roads *converge*, they come together to form one road. Starting with Sunil in the front row, I want each of you to recite a word, spell it out loud, and use it in a sentence," Mr. Maxwell said.

Sunil's word was "confess," and Timothy's heart lurched.

When it was his turn, Timothy's word was "conform."

"Conform. C-O-N-F-O-R-M. I won't conform and jump off a bridge just because everyone else is doing it," he said.

Mr. Maxwell chuckled, and then asked Josh to continue.

"Conclusive. C-O-N-C-L-U-S-I-V-E." Josh paused and smirked, and Timothy's stomach fluttered dangerously. "When we saw the ink on Marcus's hand, we had conclusive proof that he cheated during the Geography Bee," Josh finished grandly.

All around Timothy, kids snickered loudly, and Marcus went rigid—as if he'd been suddenly frozen. Mr. Maxwell frowned at Josh and sternly told him that he owed Marcus an apology.

Timothy knew that he, not Josh, was answerable to Marcus, but on the other hand, if he just stayed quiet and let Josh apologize, maybe this whole mess would go away.

Josh shuffled his feet and stared at the floor. "Marcus, I …" he muttered.

"Wait!" Timothy said, standing up—willing his legs not to tremble as a silence fell over the classroom and every head turned toward him. "Marcus didn't cheat—he won the Geography Bee fair and square, and I lied because I was jealous. I'm really sorry, Marcus."

Timothy lowered his eyes and waited. He felt so ashamed. You could have heard a clock ticking. After a long, uncomfortable moment, Mr. Maxwell cleared his throat and asked, "Marcus, do you accept Timothy's apology?"

Timothy looked over at Marcus, and tried to read his expression: did that wrinkle between his eyebrows mean he was angry … or was he just thinking?

"It's OK—I forgive you," Marcus said at last, and Timothy sighed with relief.

"Marcus, that's an excellent attitude. Well done," Mr. Maxwell said. "And Timothy, although it was wrong to lie in the first place, it took courage to own up to your mistake."

After school, Timothy hurried as fast as he could toward the bus. Marcus had been gracious in front of their teacher, but outside of the classroom, he was under no obligation to treat Timothy with kindness. Then Timothy noticed with horror that Marcus was jogging down the hallway behind him, calling his name.

"Thanks for being honest back there," Marcus said, putting a hand on Timothy's shoulder. "I know you could have just kept quiet."

"No problem," Timothy said, relaxing. "I only made up that lie because my sister won the Bee trophy a few years ago, and I wanted to show I'm just as smart as she is."

"I know how that goes—I've got two younger brothers, and my parents are always telling them how amazing they are," Marcus replied.

"Maybe you can come throw a baseball around with us sometime," Marcus continued. "Definitely not today though—looks like it's going to rain."

"Absolutely!" said Timothy, thinking of his weird dream and smiling.

Summarize

Use important details from *The Hardest Lesson* to summarize why Timothy took responsibility for his actions. Information from your graphic organizer may help.

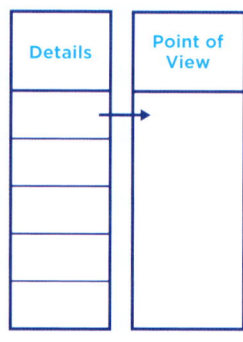

Text Evidence

1. What features tell you this is realistic fiction? **GENRE**

2. How does the narrator help you understand what the characters are thinking and feeling? **POINT OF VIEW**

3. What does "break a leg" on page 3 mean? What clues from the text helped you determine its definition? **IDIOMS**

4. *The Hardest Lesson* is written from a third-person point of view, where the narrator is limited to showing only Timothy's thoughts and feelings. Reread page 14, then write a paragraph in first person, describing the events from Marcus's point of view. **WRITE ABOUT READING**

CCSS Genre Poetry

Compare Texts
Read about how an older brother takes on the responsibility of helping a younger sister.

Training Wheels

"She's only just learning," Mom says,
"So, go slow." I nod.
Squeak squeak squeak
The training wheels chirp, and my sister whines,
"You're getting ahead of me!"
"I'm right here!" I shout. "You won't fall!"
Her bike is pink with long, thin streamers,
Which I'm sure she pictures
Flying in the wind as her wheels whirl like crazy.
Side by side, we creep up the street,
Though I could be miles ahead.
We pass our neighbor's funny yard
ornaments—flamingos,
stone lions, and gnomes
with round, rosy faces
and pointed caps.
"Look! He's got a new
one," my sister says.
"No, silly, he's had
that dancing gnome
for years."

"Come on," I say, "let's go!"
"I'm pedaling as hard as I can," she says.
It's tough to crawl along like this,
My legs are aching from the tedious motion.
With a few swift strokes I push ahead,
Picking up speed.
She's not that far behind me, I tell myself,
Less than half a block.
The grass isn't exactly a blur—
More like a steady wave,
An expanding, green ribbon.
It's a perfect day for riding,
With the sunshine, and the slight breeze.
My sister is still in view, but barely—
Soon, I can't see her moving at all.
I have to turn back and retrace old ground.
It takes me a few minutes to reach her—
Longer than I thought.

She's sitting on her bike, perfectly still,
Looking up into the oak tree. "See?"
She points to the branches, almost bare last month,
But now totally covered, as if by magic.
"They're making a home," she whispers.
I squint at the sky, and sure enough,
Two birds are flying in relay,
Carrying bits of twig and grass high into the air.
They depend on each other, you can tell.
"Ready?" my sister asks, turning to me.
"Mm-hmm," but I keep standing next to her,
Holding her bike steady.
"See if you can balance," I say.
"Too hard," she whines, but she pedals anyway,
Short, uncertain movements, becoming smoother.
I let go, and for a second,
Her training wheels lift.

Make Connections

What does the speaker of *Training Wheels* do that shows that he has taken responsibility?
ESSENTIAL QUESTION

Compare Timothy in *The Hardest Lesson* with the speaker in *Training Wheels*. How are they alike?
TEXT TO TEXT

Alliteration *Training Wheels* is a free-verse poem that explores the theme of responsibility for being a good brother. In free verse, there is no regular rhyme scheme, although the poet may add a rhyme from time to time. In free verse, the poet can use other ways to create rhythm and energy. Alliteration is one way to do this. It involves the poet repeating the first sound in a group of words; for example, "Peter Piper picked a peck of pickled peppers."

Read and Find In a number of places in the poem *Training Wheels*, the poet has used alliteration of the letter *s*. For example, on page 18, "With the sunshine, and the slight breeze. My sister is still in view …" and on page 17, "'So, go slow.' I nod. *Squeak squeak squeak*." Also on page 17, the poet uses the letter *w* in the same way: "Flying in the wind as her wheels whirl like crazy." Each example of alliteration creates a rhythm within the free-verse form of the poem.

Your Turn

Choose an event, person, or object and write a short free-verse poem explaining your thoughts and feelings. In several places in the poem, include an example of alliteration. Choose a range of letters to alliterate so you introduce a sense of rhythm into your writing. Now read your poem aloud to a partner. Ask your partner to identify each example of alliteration as he or she listens to you read.